Data Mashups in R

Data Mashups in R

Jeremy Leipzig and Xiao-Yi Li

O'REILLY®

Beijing · Cambridge · Farnham · Köln · Sebastopol · Tokyo

Data Mashups in R

by Jeremy Leipzig and Xiao-Yi Li

Published by O'Reilly Media, Inc., 1005 Gravenstein Highway North, Sebastopol, CA 95472.

O'Reilly books may be purchased for educational, business, or sales promotional use. Online editions are also available for most titles (*http://my.safaribooksonline.com*). For more information, contact our corporate/institutional sales department: (800) 998-9938 or *corporate@oreilly.com*.

Editor: Mike Loukides	**Cover Designer:** Karen Montgomery
Production Editor: Kristen Borg	**Interior Designer:** David Futato
Proofreader: Kristen Borg	**Illustrator:** Robert Romano

Printing History:

March 2011:	First Edition.

ISBN: 978-1-449-30353-2

[LSI]

1299253424

Table of Contents

Introduction

Programmers may spend a good part of their careers scripting code to conform to commercial statistics packages, visualization tools, and domain-specific third-party software. The same tasks can force end users to spend countless hours in copy-paste purgatory, each minor change necessitating another grueling round of formatting tabs and screenshots. Luckily, R scripting offers some reprieve. Because this open source project garners the support of a large community of package developers, the R statistical programming environment provides an amazing level of extensibility. Data from a multitude of sources can be imported into R and processed using R packages to aid statistical analysis and visualization. R scripts can also be configured to produce high-quality reports in an automated fashion—saving time, energy, and frustration.

This book will demonstrate how real-world data is imported, managed, visualized, and analyzed within R. Spatial mashups provide an excellent way to explore the capabilities of R—encompassing R packages, R syntax, and data structures. Instead of canned sample data, we will be plotting and analyzing actual current home foreclosure auctions. Through this exercise, we hope to provide an general idea of how the R environment works with R packages as well as its own capabilities in statistical analysis. We will be accessing spatial data in several formats (HTML, XML, shapefiles, and text) both locally and over the web, to produce a map of home foreclosures and perform statistical analysis on these events.

CHAPTER 1

Mapping Foreclosures

Messy Address Parsing

To illustrate how to combine data from disparate sources for statistical analysis and visualization, let's focus on one of the messiest sources of data around: web pages.

The Philadelphia sheriff's office posts foreclosure auctions on its website (*http://www .phillysheriff.com/properties.html*) each month. How do we collect this data, massage it into a reasonable form, and work with it? First, create a new folder (for example, *~/ Rmashup*) to contain our project files. It is helpful to change the R working directory to your newly created folder.

```
#In Unix/MacOS
> setwd("~/Documents/Rmashup/")
#In Windows
> setwd("C:/~/Rmashup/")
```

We can download this foreclosure listings web page from within R (or you may instead choose to save the raw HTML from your web browser):

```
> download.file(url="http://www.phillysheriff.com/properties.html",
    destfile="properties.html")
```

Here is some of this web page's source HTML, with addresses highlighted:

```
6321 Farnsworth St.
      62nd                                        Ward
1,379.88 sq. ft.  BRT# 621533500  Improvements: Residential Property
<br><b>
HOMER SIMPSON
    
</b>  C.P. January Term, 2006  No. 002619     $27,537.87
      Phelan Hallinan & Schmieg, L.L.P.
 <hr />
<center><b>      243-467              </b></center>
1402 E. Mt. Pleasant Ave.
       50th                                       Ward
approximately 1,416 sq. ft. more or less  BRT# 502440300 ...
```

The sheriff's raw HTML listings are inconsistently formatted, but with the right regular expression we can identify street addresses: notice how they appear alone on a line. Our goal is to submit viable addresses to the geocoder. Here are some typical addresses that our regular expression should match:

```
3509 N. Lee St.
2120-2128 E. Allegheny Ave.
7601 Crittenden St., #E-10
370 Tomlinson Place
2311 N. 33rd St.
6822-24 Old York Rd.
335 W. School House Lane
```

These are not addresses and should not be matched:

```
2,700 sq. ft.  BRT# 124077100  Improvements: Residential Property
</b> C.P. June Term, 2009  No. 00575        
```

R has built-in functions that allow the use of Perl-type regular expressions. For more info on regular expressions, see Mastering Regular Expressions (O'Reilly) and Regular Expression Pocket Reference (O'Reilly).

With some minor deletions to clean up address idiosyncrasies, we should be able to correctly identify street addresses from the mess of other data contained in *properties.html*. We'll use a single regular expression pattern to do the cleanup. For clarity, we can break the pattern into the familiar elements of an address (number, name, suffix)

```
> stNum<-"^[0-9]{2,5}(\\-[0-9]+)?"
> stName<-"([NSEW]\\. )?[0-9A-Z ]+"
> stSuf<-"(St|Ave|Place|Blvd|Drive|Lane|Ln|Rd)(\\.?)$"
> myStPat<-paste(stNum,stName,stSuf,sep=" ")
```

Note the backslash characters themselves must be escaped with a backslash to avoid conflict with R syntax. Let's test this pattern against our examples using R's grep() function:

```
> grep(myStPat,"6822-24 Old York Rd.",perl=TRUE,value=FALSE,ignore.case=TRUE)
[1] 1
> grep(myStPat,"2,700 sq. ft.  BRT# 124077100  Improvements: Residential Property",
        perl=TRUE,value=FALSE,ignore.case=TRUE)
integer(0)
```

The result, [1] 1, shows that the first of our target address strings matched; we tested only one string at a time. We also have to omit strings that we don't want with our address, such as extra punctuation (like quotes or commas), or sheriff's office designations that follow street names:

```
> badStrings<-"(\\r| a\\/?[kd]\\/?a.+$| - Premise.+$| assessed as.+$|,
  Unit.+|<font size=\"[0-9]\">|Apt\\..+| #.+$|[,\"]|\\s+$)"
```

Test this against some examples using R's gsub() function:

```
> gsub(badStrings,'',"119 Hagy's Mill Rd. a/k/a 119 Spring Lane",
        perl=TRUE)
[1] "119 Hagy's Mill Rd."
> gsub(badStrings,'',"3229 Hurley St. - Premise A",perl=TRUE)
[1] "3229 Hurley St."
```

Let's encapsulate this address parsing into a function that will accept an HTML file and return a vector, a one-dimensional ordered collection with a specific data type, in this case character. Copy and paste this entire block into your R console:

```
#input:html filename
#returns:data frame of geocoded addresses that can be plotted by PBSmapping
getAddressesFromHTML<-function(myHTMLDoc){
  myStreets<-vector(mode="character",0)
  stNum<-"^[0-9]{2,5}(\\-[0-9]+)?"
  stName<-"([NSEW]\\. )?([0-9A-Z ]+)"
  stSuf<-"(St|Ave|Place|Blvd|Drive|Lane|Ln|Rd)(\\.?)$"
  badStrings<-paste(
    "(\\r| a\\/?[kd]\\/?a.+$| - Premise.+$| assessed as.+$|,",
    "Unit.+|<font size=\"[0-9]\">|Apt\\..+| #.+$|[,\"]|\\s+$)")
  myStPat<-paste(stNum,stName,stSuf,sep=" ")
  for(line in readLines(myHTMLDoc)){
    line<-gsub(badStrings,'',line,perl=TRUE)
    matches<-grep(myStPat,line,perl=TRUE,
                  value=FALSE,ignore.case=TRUE)
    if(length(matches)>0){
      myStreets<-append(myStreets,line)
    }
  }
  myStreets
}
```

We can test this function on our downloaded HTML file:

```
> streets<-getAddressesFromHTML("properties.html")
> length(streets)
[1] 1264
```

Exploring "streets"

R has very strong support for vector subscripting. To access the first six foreclosures on our list:

```
> streets[1:6]
[1] "6321 Farnsworth St."    "5711 Anderson St."      "1250 S. 24th St."
[4] "1546 S. 26th St."       "2401 Pennsylvania Ave." "812 S. 58th St."
```

c() forms a vector from its arguments. Subscripting a vector with another vector does what you'd expect—here's how to form a vector from the first and last elements of the list:

```
> streets[c(1,length(streets))]
[1] "6321 Farnsworth St." "7455 Ruskin Rd."
```

Here's how to select foreclosures that are on a "Place":

```
> streets[grep("Place",streets)]
[1] "1430 Dondill Place"   "370 Tomlinson Place" "8025 Pompey Place"
[4] "7330 Boreal Place"    "2818 Ryerson Place"  "8416 Suffolk Place"
```

To order foreclosures by street number, dispense with non-numeric characters, cast as numeric, and use order() to get the indices.

```
> streets[order(as.numeric(gsub("[^0-9].+",'',streets)))]
   [1] "21 S. 51st St."       "22 E. Garfield St."
   [3] "26 W. Manheim St."    "26 N. Felton St."
   [5] "30 S. 58th St."       "31 N. Columbus Blvd."
   ...
[1259] "12122 Barbary Rd."    "12223 Medford Rd."
[1261] "12430 Wyndom Rd."     "12701 Medford Rd."
[1263] "12727 Medford Rd."    "13054 Townsend Rd."
```

Obtaining Latitude and Longitude Using Yahoo

To plot our foreclosures on a map, we'll need to get latitude and longitude coordinates for each street address. Yahoo Maps provides this functionality (called "geocoding") as a REST-enabled web service. Via HTTP, the service accepts a URL containing a partial or full street address, and returns an XML document with the relevant information. It doesn't matter whether a web browser or a robot is submitting the request, as long as the URL is correctly formatted. The URL must contain an appid parameter and as many street address arguments as are known.

http://local.yahooapis.com/MapsService/V1/geocode?appid=YD-9G7bey8 _JXxQP6rxl.fBFGgCdNjoDMACQA--&street=1+South+Broad+St&city=Philadel phia&state=PA

In response we get:

```
<?xml version="1.0"?>
<ResultSet xmlns:xsi="http://www.w3.org/2001/XMLSchema-instance"
xmlns="urn:yahoo:maps"
xsi:schemaLocation=
"urn:yahoo:maps http://api.local.yahoo.com/MapsService/V1/GeocodeResponse.xsd">
<Result precision="address">
<Latitude>39.951405</Latitude>
<Longitude>-75.163735</Longitude>
<Address>1 S Broad St</Address>
<City>Philadelphia</City>
<State>PA</State>
<Zip>19107-3300</Zip>
<Country>US</Country>
</Result>
</ResultSet>
```

To use this service with your mashup, you must sign up with Yahoo! and receive an Application ID. Use that ID in with the `appid` parameter of the request URL. You can sign up at *http://developer.yahoo.com/wsregapp/*.

Shaking the XML Tree

Parsing well-formed and valid XML should be less convoluted than parsing the sheriff's HTML. An XML parsing package is available for R; here's how to install it from CRAN's repository:

```
> install.packages("XML")
> library("XML")
```

If you are behind a firewall or proxy and getting errors:

On Unix, set your *http_proxy* environment variable.

On Windows, try the custom install R wizard with the "internet2" option instead of "standard". You can find additional information at *http://cran.r-project.org/bin/windows/base/rw-FAQ.html#The-Internet-download-functions-fail_00*.

Our goal is to extract values contained within the <Latitude> and <Longitude> leaf nodes. These nodes live within the <Result> node, which lives inside a <ResultSet> node, which itself lies inside the root node.

To find an appropriate library for getting these values, call `library(help=XML)`. This function lists the functions in the XML package.

```
> library(help=XML)  #hit space to scroll, q to exit
> ?xmlTreeParse
```

You'll see that the function `xmlTreeParse` will accept an XML file or URL and return an R structure. After inserting your Yahoo App ID, paste in this block:

```
> library(XML)
> appid<-'<put your appid here>'
> street<-"1 South Broad Street"
> requestUrl<-paste(
  "http://local.yahooapis.com/MapsService/V1/geocode?appid=",
  appid,
  "&street=",
  URLencode(street),
  "&city=Philadelphia&state=PA"
  ,sep="")
> xmlResult<-xmlTreeParse(requestUrl,isURL=TRUE)
```

Are you behind a Windows firewall or proxy and this example is giving you trouble?

xmlTreeParse has no respect for your proxy settings. Do the following:

```
> Sys.setenv("http_proxy" = "http://myProxyServer:myProxyPort")
```

or if you use a username/password:

```
> Sys.setenv("http_proxy"="http://username:password@proxyHost:proxyPort")
```

You need to install the cURL package to handle fetching web pages:

```
> install.packages("RCurl")
> library("RCurl")
```

In the example above, change:

```
> xmlResult<-xmlTreeParse(requestUrl,isURL=TRUE)
```

to:

```
> xmlResult<-xmlTreeParse(getURL(requestUrl))
```

The XML package can perform event- or tree-based parsing. However, because we only need two bits of information (latitude and longitude), we can go straight for the jugular by gleaning what we can from the data structure that xmlTreeParse returns:

```
> str(xmlResult)
List of 2
 $ doc:List of 3
  ..$ file     :List of 1
  .. ..$ Result:List of 7
  .. .. ..$ Latitude :List of 1
  .. .. .. ..$ text: list()
  .. .. .. .. ..- attr(*, "class")= chr [1:5] "XMLTextNode" "XMLNode" "RXMLAb...
  .. .. .. ..- attr(*, "class")= chr [1:4] "XMLNode" "RXMLAbstractNode" "XMLA...
  .. .. ..$ Longitude:List of 1
  .. .. .. ..$ text: list()
  .. .. .. .. ..- attr(*, "class")= chr [1:5] "XMLTextNode" "XMLNode" "RXMLAb...
  .. .. .. ..- attr(*, "class")= chr [1:4] "XMLNode" "RXMLAbstractNode" "XMLA...
(snip)
```

That's kind of a mess, but we can see that our Longitude and Latitude are Lists inside of Lists inside of a List inside of a List.

Tom Short's R reference card, an invaluable resource (available at *http://cran.r-project.org/doc/contrib/Short-refcard.pdf*), tells us to get the name element in list x of a list in R: x[["name"]].

The Many Ways to Philly (Latitude)

There are three different ways we can extract the latitude and longitude coordinates from our XML result.

Using Data Structures

Using the indexing list notation from R, we can get to the nodes we need:

```
> lat<-xmlResult[['doc']][['ResultSet']][['Result']][['Latitude']][['text']]
> long<-xmlResult[['doc']][['ResultSet']][['Result']][['Longitude']][['text']]

> lat
39.951405
```

This looks good, but examine this further:

```
> str(lat)
list()
- attr(*, "class")= chr [1:5] "XMLTextNode" "XMLNode" "RXMLAbstractNode" "XML...
```

Although it has a decent *display value*, this variable still considers itself an XMLNode and contains no index to obtain the raw leaf value we want—the descriptor just says list() instead of something we can use (like $lat). We're not quite there yet.

Using Helper Methods

Fortunately, the XML package offers a method to access the leaf value—xmlValue:

```
> lat<-xmlValue(xmlResult[['doc']][['ResultSet']][['Result']][['Latitude']])

> str(lat)
chr "39.951405"
```

Using Internal Class Methods

There are usually multiple ways to accomplish the same task in R. Another means to get to our character lat/long data is to use the value method provided by the node itself:

```
> lat<-xmlResult[['doc']][['ResultSet']][['Result']][['Latitude']][['text']]$value
```

If we were really clever, we would have understood that the XML doc class provided us with useful methods all the way down! Try neurotically holding down the tab key after typing this:

```
> lat<-xmlResult$  (now hold down the tab key)

xmlResult$doc   xmlResult$dtd
(let's go with doc and start looking for more methods using $)

> lat<-xmlResult$doc$
```

With enough experimentation, we can get all the way to the result we are looking for:

```
> lat<-xmlResult$doc$children$ResultSet$children
               $Result$children$Latitude$children$text$value

> str(lat)
chr "39.951405"
```

We get the same usable result using raw data structures with helper methods, or internal object methods. In a more complex or longer tree structure, we might have also used event-based or XPath-style parsing to get to our value. You should always begin by trying the approaches that you find most intuitive.

Exceptional Circumstances

To ensure that our script runs smoothly, we need to deal with the possibility that an address cannot be geocoded or that our conversation with the geocoder will be interrupted.

The Unmappable Fake Street

Now we have to deal with the problem of bad street addresses—either the sheriff's office entered a typo or our parser let a bad street address pass (see *http://local.yahooapis .com/MapsService/V1/geocode?appid=YD-9G7bey8_JXxQP6rxl.fBFGgCdNjoD MACQA--&street=1+Fake+St&city=Philadelphia&state=PA*).

The Yahoo documentation states that when confronted with an address that cannot be mapped, the geocoder will return coordinates pointing to the center of the city. Note the precision attribute of the result is **"zip"** instead of **address** and there is a **warning** attribute as well:

```
<?xml version="1.0"?>
<ResultSet xmlns:xsi="http://www.w3.org/2001/XMLSchema-instance"
 xmlns="urn:yahoo:maps"
 xsi:schemaLocation=
"urn:yahoo:maps http://api.local.yahoo.com/MapsService/V1/GeocodeResponse.xsd">
<Result precision="zip"
 warning="The street could not be found. Here is the center of the city.">
<Latitude>39.952270</Latitude>
<Longitude>-75.162369</Longitude>
<Address>
</Address>
<City>Philadelphia</City>
<State>PA</State>
<Zip></Zip>
<Country>US</Country>
</Result>
</ResultSet>
```

Paste in the following:

```
> street<-"1 Fake St"
> requestUrl<-paste(
    "http://local.yahooapis.com/MapsService/V1/geocode?appid=",
    appid,
    "&street=",
    URLencode(street),
    "&city=Philadelphia&state=PA"
    ,sep="")
```

We need to get a hold of the *attribute* tags within <Result> to distinguish bad geocoding events, or else we could accidentally record events in the center of the city as foreclosures. By reading the RSXML FAQ (*http://www.omegahat.org/RSXML/FAQ.html*), it becomes clear we need to turn on the addAttributeNamespaces parameter to our xmlTreeParse call if we are to see the precision tag:

```
> xmlResult<-xmlTreeParse(requestUrl,isURL=TRUE,addAttributeNamespaces=TRUE)
```

Now we can dig down to get that precision tag, which is an element of $attributes, a named list:

```
> xmlResult$doc$children$ResultSet$children$Result$attributes['precision']
precision
"zip"
```

We can add this condition to our geocoding function:

```
> if(xmlResult$doc$children$ResultSet$children
     $Result$attributes['precision'] == 'address'){
    cat("I have address precision!\n")
  }else{
    cat("I don't know where this is!\n")
  }
```

No Connection

Finally we need to account for unforeseen exceptions—such as losing our Internet connection or the Yahoo web service failing to respond. It is not uncommon for this free service to drop out when bombarded by requests. A tryCatch clause will alert us if this does happen and prevent bad data from getting into our results.

```
> tryCatch({
      xmlResult<-xmlTreeParse(requestUrl,isURL=TRUE,addAttributeNamespaces=TRUE)
      #...other code...
  }, error=function(err){
      cat("xml parsing or http error:", conditionMessage(err), "\n")
  })
```

We will compile all this code into a single function once we know how to merge it with a map (see "Developing the Plot" on page 11).

Taking Shape

To display a map of Philadelphia with our foreclosures, we need to find a polygon of the county as well as a means of plotting our lat/long coordinates onto it. Both of these requirements are met by the ubiquitous ESRI shapefile format. The term shapefile collectively refers to a *.shp* file (which contains polygons), and related files that store other features, indices, and metadata.

Finding a Usable Map

Googling "philadelphia shapefile" returns several promising results including this page: *http://www.temple.edu/ssdl/Shape_files.htm*.

The "Philadelphia Tracts" maps on that website seem useful because they include US Census Tract information. We can use these tract IDs to link to other census data. Tracts are standardized to contain roughly 1500-8000 people, so densely populated tracts tend to be smaller. This particular shapefile is especially appealing because the map "projection" uses the same WGS84 (*http://en.wikipedia.org/wiki/World_Geodetic _System*) Lat/Long coordinate system that our address geocoding service uses, as opposed to a "state plane coordinate system," which can be difficult to transform. Transformations require the rgdal package (*http://cran.r-project.org/web/packages/rgdal/in dex.html*) and GDAL executables (*http://www.gdal.org/*).

Save and unzip the following file to your project directory: *http://www.temple.edu/ssdl/ shpfiles/phila_tracts_2000.zip*.

PBSmapping

PBSmapping is a popular R package that offers several means of interacting with spatial data. It relies on some base functions from the maptools package to read ESRI shapefiles, so we need both packages:

```
> install.packages(c("maptools","PBSmapping"))
```

As with other packages, we can see the functions using library(help=PBSmapping) and view function descriptions using ?topic: (see *http://cran.r-project.org/web/packages/ PBSmapping/index.html*).

We can use str to examine the structure of the shapefile imported by PBS mapping::importShapeFile:

```
> library(PBSmapping)

PBS Mapping 2.61.9 -- Copyright (C) 2003-2010 Fisheries and Oceans Canada

-----------------------------------------------------------
PBS Mapping comes with ABSOLUTELY NO WARRANTY;
for details see the file COPYING.
This is free software, and you are welcome to redistribute
it under certain conditions, as outlined in the above file.
-----------------------------------------------------------

A complete user guide 'PBSmapping-UG.pdf' is located at
 /Library/Frameworks/R.framework/Versions/2.12/Resources/library/ \
  PBSmapping/doc/PBSmapping-UG.pdf

To see demos, type '.PBSfigs()'.
```

Packaged on 2010-06-23
Pacific Biological Station, Nanaimo

```
> myShapeFile<-importShapefile("tracts2000",readDBF=TRUE)

Loading required package: maptools
Loading required package: foreign
Loading required package: sp

> str(myShapeFile)
Classes 'PolySet' and 'data.frame':    16290 obs. of  5 variables:
$ PID: int  1 1 1 1 1 1 1 1 1 ...
$ SID: int  1 1 1 1 1 1 1 1 1 ...
$ POS: int  1 2 3 4 5 6 7 8 9 10 ...
$ X  : num  -75.2 -75.2 -75.2 -75.2 -75.2 ...
$ Y  : num  39.9 39.9 39.9 40 40 ...
 - attr(*, "PolyData")=Classes 'PolyData' and 'data.frame': 381 obs. of 9 var...
 ..$ PID     : int  1 2 3 4 5 6 7 8 9 10 ...
 ..$ ID      : Factor w/ 381 levels "1","10","100",..: 1 112 223 316 327 338...
 ..$ FIPSSTCO: Factor w/ 1 level "42101": 1 1 1 1 1 1 1 1 1 ...
 ..$ TRT2000 : Factor w/ 381 levels "000100","000200",..: 1 2 3 4 5 6 7 8 9 ...
 ..$ STFID   : Factor w/ 381 levels "42101000100",..: 1 2 3 4 5 6 7 8 9 10 ...
 ..$ TRACTID : Factor w/ 381 levels "1","10","100",..: 1 114 226 313 327 337...
 ..$ PARK    : num  0 0 0 0 0 0 0 0 0 ...
 ..$ OLDID   : num  1 1 1 1 1 1 1 1 1 ...
 ..$ NEWID   : num  2 2 2 2 2 2 2 2 2 ...
 - attr(*, "parent.child")= num  1 1 1 1 1 1 1 1 1 ...
 - attr(*, "shpType")= int 5
 - attr(*, "prj")= chr "Unknown"
 - attr(*, "projection")= num 1
```

While the shapefile itself consists of 16290 points that make up Philadelphia, it appears that much of the polygon data associated with this shapefile is stored as an attribute of myShapeFile. We should set that to a top level variable for easier access:

```
> myPolyData<-attr(myShapeFile,"PolyData")
```

Plotting this shapefile is a one-liner (see Figure 1-1):

```
> plotPolys(myShapeFile)
```

Let's spruce that up a bit (see Figure 1-2):

```
> plotPolys(myShapeFile,axes=FALSE,bg="beige",main="Philadelphia County\n
        January 2011 Foreclosures",xlab="",ylab="")
```

Developing the Plot

With foreclosures represented as geographic coordinates, the addPoints function in the PBSmapping package can plot each foreclosure as a point on the shapefile, provided the function is given a properly formatted data frame object.

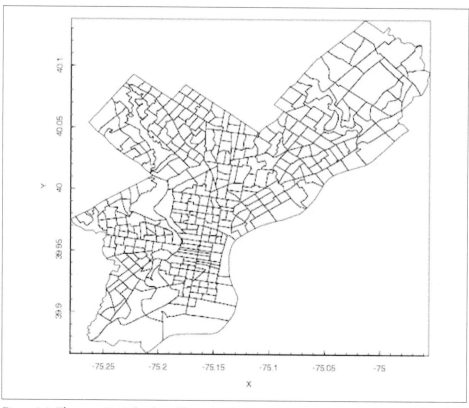

Figure 1-1. The tracts2000.shp shapefile rendered by plotPolys

Preparing to Add Points to Our Map

To use the PBSmapping's `addPoints` function, the reference manual suggests that we treat our foreclosures as `EventData`. The `EventData` format is a standard R data frame (more on data frames later) with required columns X, Y, and a unique row identifier, an event ID (EID). With this in mind, we can write a function around our geocoding code that will accept a list of streets and return a kosher `EventData`-like data frame:

```
#input:vector of streets
#output:data frame containing lat/longs in PBSmapping-like format
> geocodeAddresses<-function(myStreets){
    appid<-'<put your appid here>'
    myGeoTable<-data.frame(
    address=character(),lat=numeric(),long=numeric(),EID=numeric())
  for(myStreet in myStreets){
    requestUrl<-paste(
    "http://local.yahooapis.com/MapsService/V1/geocode?appid=",
    appid,
    "&street=",URLencode(myStreet),
    "&city=Philadelphia&state=PA",sep="")
    cat("geocoding:",myStreet,"\n")
```

```
    tryCatch({
      xmlResult<-
        xmlTreeParse(requestUrl,isURL=TRUE,addAttributeNamespaces=TRUE)
      geoResult<-xmlResult$doc$children$ResultSet$children$Result
      if(geoResult$attributes['precision'] == 'address'){
        lat<-xmlValue(geoResult[['Latitude']])
        long<-xmlValue(geoResult[['Longitude']])
        myGeoTable<-rbind(myGeoTable,
          data.frame(address = myStreet, Y = lat, X   =
          long,EID=NA))
      }
    }, error=function(err){
      cat("xml parsing/http error:", conditionMessage(err), "\n")
    })
    Sys.sleep(0.5) #this pause helps keep Yahoo happy
  }
  #use built-in numbering as the event id for PBSmapping
  myGeoTable$EID<-as.numeric(rownames(myGeoTable))
  myGeoTable
}
```

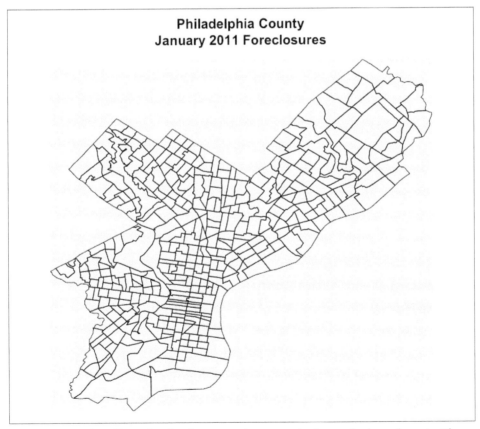

Figure 1-2. The shapefile rendered without axes, given a new background color and a main title

After pasting the above geocodeAddresses function into your R console, enter in the following (make sure you still have a streets vector from the parsing chapter):

```
> geoTable<-geocodeAddresses(streets) geocoding: 410 N. 61st St.
geocoding: 6321 Farnsworth St.
geocoding: 5711 Anderson St.
geocoding: 1250 S. 24th St.
geocoding: 1546 S. 26th St.
geocoding: 2401 Pennsylvania Ave.
geocoding: 812 S. 58th St.
geocoding: 3509 N. Lee St.
...(10 minutes later)...
gecoding: 7455 Ruskin Rd.
```

Exploring R Data Structures: geoTable

A data frame is R's interpretation of a spreadsheet:

```
> names(geoTable)
[1] "address" "Y"        "X"         "EID"
> nrow(geoTable)
 [1] 1264
```

The first row:

```
> geoTable[1,]
             address         Y          X EID
1 6321 Farnsworth St. 40.032400 -75.067243   1
```

X and Y from the first five rows:

```
> geoTable[1:5,c("X","Y")]
          X         Y
1 -75.067243 40.032400
2 -75.159509 40.051511
3 -75.183899 39.937076
4 -75.188141 39.933655
5 -75.177794 39.966036
```

The cell in the 4th column, 4th row:

```
> geoTable[4,4]
[1] 4
```

The second column, also known as "Y":

```
> geoTable[,2]
    #or#
> geoTable$Y

 [1] 40.032400 40.051511 39.937076 39.933655 39.966036 39.948570 40.003219 40.011250
 [9] 39.975206 39.999268 39.997490 39.993409 39.978768 39.991603 39.987332 39.992144
 ...
```

Making Events of Our Foreclosures

Our geoTable is similar in structure to an EventData object but we need to use the as.EventData function to complete the conversion.

```
> addressEvents<-as.EventData(geoTable,projection=NA)
Error in as.EventData(geoTable, projection = NA) :
  Cannot coerce into EventData.
One or more columns contains factors where they are not allowed.
Columns that cannot contain factors: EID, X, Y.
```

Oh snap! The dreaded "factor feature" in R strikes again. When a data frame column contains factors (*http://cran.r-project.org/doc/manuals/R-lang.html#Factors*), its elements are represented using indices that refer to levels, distinct values within that column. The as.EventData method is expecting columns of type numeric, not factor. *Never* transform from factors to numeric like this:

```
as.numeric(myTable$factorColumn) #don't do this!
```

This is an extremely common mistake—this will merely return numeric indices used to refer to the levels—but you want the levels themselves:

```
> geoTable$X<-as.numeric(levels(geoTable$X))[geoTable$X] #do this
> geoTable$Y<-as.numeric(levels(geoTable$Y))[geoTable$Y]
```

With numeric lat/longs in hand, we can quantitatively explore this geographic data. What is the northernmost (highest latitude) of our foreclosures?

```
> geoTable[geoTable$Y==max(geoTable$Y),]
                 address        Y        X  EID
1151 100 County Line Rd. 40.13754 -75.0145 1151
```

The EventData casting should work now that our columns are numeric.

```
> addressEvents<-as.EventData(geoTable,projection=NA)
> addPoints(addressEvents,col="red",cex=.5)
```

The EventData is rendered as tiny circles using addPoints (see Figure 1-3).

Turning Up the Heat

PBSmapping allows us to see in which polygons/tracts our foreclosures were plotted. Using this data, we can represent the intensity of foreclosure events as a heatmap. We can use the head function to inspect the first few rows of a data frame:

```
> addressPolys<-findPolys(addressEvents,myShapeFile)
> head(addressPolys)
   EID PID SID Bdry
1   37   1   1    0
2  780   1   1    0
3  781   1   1    0
4 1164   1   1    0
5 1178   1   1    0
6 1179   1   1    0
```

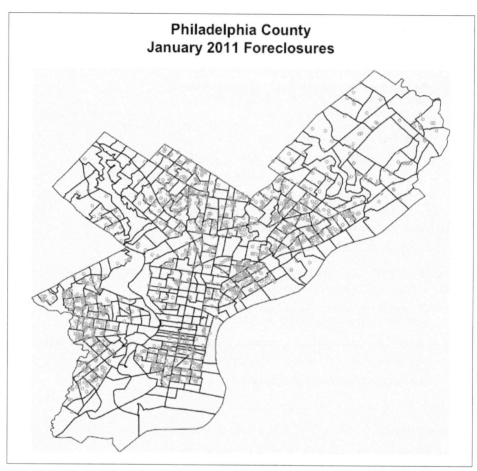

Figure 1-3. The shapefile with address events added as points

Factors When You Need Them

Each EID (event ID, or foreclosure) is associated with a PID (polygon ID, or tract). To plot our heatmap, we need to count instances of PIDs in addressPolys for each tract on the map.

```
> length(levels(as.factor(myShapeFile$PID)))
[1] 381

> length(levels(as.factor(addressPolys$PID)))
[1] 290
```

We can see that there are 381 census tracts in Philadelphia County, but only 290 have foreclosure events. For the purpose of coloring our polygons, we need to ensure that the remainder of the tracts are explicitly set to 0 foreclosures.

The table function in R can be used to make this sort of contingency table. We need a variable, myTrtFC, to hold the number of foreclosures in each tract/PID:

```
> myTrtFC<-
  table(factor(addressPolys$PID,levels=levels(as.factor(myShapeFile$PID))))
> head(myTrtFC)
1 2 3 4 5 6
7 3 0 1 0 0
```

To enforce our new levels, we must use a constructor (factor) instead of a variable conversion (as.factor).

Filling with Color Gradients

R has some decent built-in color gradient functions (enter ?rainbow to learn more)—we will need a different color for each non-zero level, plus one extra color for zero foreclosures:

```
> mapColors<-heat.colors(max(myTrtFC)+1,alpha=.6)[max(myTrtFC)-myTrtFC+1]
```

Our plot is virtually the same, but we need to add the color vector argument (col). We can also easily add a legend with a sequence for 16 through 0 foreclosures and corresponding heat levels (Figure 1-4), and resize the legend with the cex argument:

```
> plotPolys(myShapeFile,axes=FALSE,bg="beige",main="Philadelphia County\n
           January 2011 Foreclosure Heat Map",xlab="",ylab="",col=mapColors)
> legend("bottomright",legend=max(myTrtFC):0,
  fill=heat.colors(max(myTrtFC)+1,alpha=.6),cex=.7,
  title="Foreclosures")
```

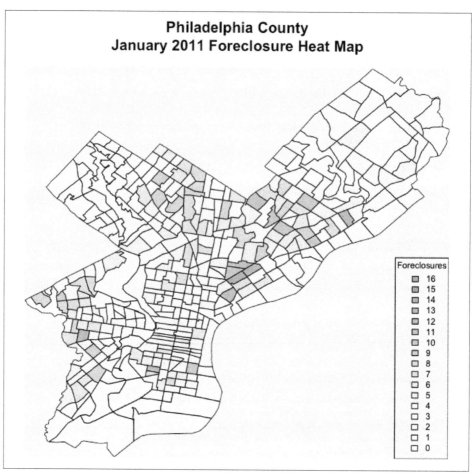

Figure 1-4. The shapefile with tracts filled using a color gradient

CHAPTER 2

Statistics of Foreclosure

Importing Census Data

The same parsing, rendering of shapefiles, and geocoding of foreclosure events reviewed up to this point can be done in a number of other platforms. The real strength of R is found in its extensive statistical functions and libraries.

The US Census Bureau collects an extensive range of socioeconomic data that are interesting for our purposes. We can download some data pertaining to total population and total housing units that are indexed by the same tracts we have used for our map. The FactFinder download center (*http://factfinder.census.gov/servlet/DCGeoSelectServ let?ds_name=DEC_2000_SF3_U*) provides easy access to this data, as shown in Figure 2-1.

Then, select All Census Tracts in a County→Pennsylvania→Philadelphia County→ Selected Detailed Tables, as shown in Figure 2-2.

Add the eight tables (P1,P13, P14, P31, P41, P53, P87,H33), click Next, download the file, and unzip it.

Figure 2-1. The Census Bureau page containing all census tracts data; Pennsylvania and Philadelphia County are selected from the drop-down menu

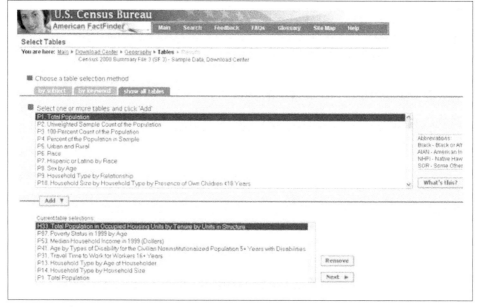

Figure 2-2. The Census Bureau page showing all available titles in the Philadelphia County region

Import this data into R, and use the function str() to see the data contained in each column:

```
> censusTable1<-read.table("dc_dec_2000_sf3_u_geo.txt",sep="|",header=TRUE)
> censusTable2<-read.table("dc_dec_2000_sf3_u_data1.txt",sep="|", header=TRUE,
                           skip=1, na.string="")
> colnames(censusTable2)
 [1] "Geography.Identifier"
 [2] "Geography.Identifier.1"
 [3] "Geographic.Summary.Level"
 [4] "Geography"
 [5] "Total.population..Total"
 [6] "Households..Total"
 [7] "Households..Family.households"
 [8] "Households..Family.households..Householder.15.to.24.years"
 [9] "Households..Family.households..Householder.25.to.34.years"
[10] "Households..Family.households..Householder.35.to.44.years"
[11] "Households..Family.households..Householder.45.to.54.years"
[12] "Households..Family.households..Householder.55.to.64.years"
[13] "Households..Family.households..Householder.65.to.74.years"
[14] "Households..Family.households..Householder.75.to.84.years"
[15] "Households..Family.households..Householder.85.years"...
```

Examining our downloaded data, we see that the first line in the text file are IDs that makes little sense, while the second line describes those IDs. The skip=1 option in read.table allow us to skip the first column, By skipping the first line, the headers of censusTable are extracted from the second line. Also keep one of R's quirks in mind—it likes to replace spaces with a period.

The columns we need are in different tables. CensusTable1 contains the tracts, Census Table2 has all the interesting survey variables, while FCs and polyData have foreclosure and shape information. The str() and merge() function can be quite useful in this case. The Geography.Identifier.1 in the censusTable2 looks familiar—it matches with STFID from the PolyData table extracted from our shapefile:

```
> str(myPolyData)
Classes 'PolyData' and 'data.frame':    381 obs. of  9 variables:
 $ PID     : int  1 2 3 4 5 6 7 8 9 10 ...
 $ ID      : Factor w/ 381 levels "1","10","100",..: 1 112 223 316 327 ...
 $ FIPSSTCO: Factor w/ 1 level "42101": 1 1 1 1 1 1 1 1 1 1 ...
 $ TRT2000 : Factor w/ 381 levels "000100","000200",..: 1 2 3 4 5 6 7 ...
 $ STFID   : Factor w/ 381 levels "42101000100",..: 1 2 3 4 5 6 7 8 9 10 ...
(snip)
#selecting columns with interesting data
> ct1<-censusTable2[,c(1,2,5,6,7,16,42,54,56,75,76,77,93,94,105)]
#merge function can merge two tables at a time
> ct2<-merge(x=censusTable1,y=myPolyData, by.x='GEO_ID2', by.y='STFID')
> ct3<-merge(x=ct2, y=ct1, by.x='GEO_ID2', by.y='Geography.Identifier.1')
```

Now we have a connection between the tracts and our census data. We also need to include the foreclosure data. We have myTrtFC, but it would be easier to do another merge if it was a data frame:

```
> myTrtFC<-as.data.frame(myTrtFC)
> names(myTrtFC)<-c("PID","FCs")
> ct<-merge(x=ct3,y=myTrtFC,by.x="PID",by.y="PID")
```

Changing the names for each column will facilitate scripting later on. Of course, it's just a personal preference:

```
> colnames(ct)<-c("PID", "GEO_ID", "GEO_ID2", "SUMLEV", "GEONAME", "GEOCOMP",
    "STATE", "COUNTY", "TRACT", "STATEP00", "COUNTYP00", "TRACTCE00", "NAME00",
    "NAMELSAD00", "MTFCC00", "FUNCSTAT00", "Geography.Identifier", "totalPop",
    "totalHousehold", "familyHousehold", "nonfamilyHousehold", "TravelTime",
    "TravelTime90+minutes", "totalDisabled", "medianHouseholdIncome",
    "povertyStatus", "BelowPoverty","OccupiedHousing", "ownedOccupied",
    "rentOccupied", "FCS")
```

Descriptive Statistics

The calculation of mean, median, and standard deviation is performed with mean(), median(), and sd(), respectively. To generate a overview of each column of a data frame summary():

```
> summary(ct)
      PID              GEO_ID                    GEO_ID2        SUMLEV
 Min.   :  1    Min.   :4.21e+10    14000US42101000100:  1    Min.   :140
 1st Qu.: 96    1st Qu.:4.21e+10    14000US42101000200:  1    1st Qu.:140
 Median :191    Median :4.21e+10    14000US42101000300:  1    Median :140
 Mean   :191    Mean   :4.21e+10    14000US42101000400:  1    Mean   :140
 3rd Qu.:286    3rd Qu.:4.21e+10    14000US42101000500:  1    3rd Qu.:140
 Max.   :381    Max.   :4.21e+10    14000US42101000600:  1    Max.   :140
```

(snip)

```
> sd(ct, na.rm=TRUE)
```
#na.rm=TRUE is necessary if there are missing data
#in the standard deviation calculations.
#The size will be only available data.
```
           PID           GEO_ID         GEO_ID2        SUMLEV
   1.101295e+02     1.075777e+04              NA   0.000000e+00
       GEONAME          GEOCOMP           STATE        COUNTY
            NA     0.000000e+00    0.000000e+00   0.000000e+00
         TRACT         STATEP00       COUNTYP00     TRACTCE00
   1.075777e+04     1.101295e+02    0.000000e+00   1.075777e+04
```
(snip)

Not all of the columns will return a numeric value, especially if it's missing. For example, MTFCC00 returns a NA. Its type is considered as a factor, as opposed to a num or int (see output from str() above). The na.rm=TRUE in the sd function removes missing data. It also follows a warning :

```
Warning messages:
  1: In var(as.vector(x), na.rm = na.rm) : NAs introduced by coercion
```

The warning serves to alert the user that the column is not of num or int type. Of course, the standard deviations of MTFCC00 or FUNCSTAT00 are nonsensical, and therefore uninteresting to calculate. In this case, we can ignore the warning message.

Let's look at two more descriptive statistics, correlation and frequency:

```
> cor(ct[,c(18,19)], method="pearson", use="complete")
               totalPop totalHousehold
totalPop      1.0000000      0.9156951
totalHousehold 0.9156951      1.0000000
```

cor has a default method using Pearson's test statistic, calculating the shortest "distance" between each of the pairwise variables. Total population and household families are very close to each other, and thus have a R-squared value of 0.92. The use="com plete" option suggests that only those variables with no missing values should be used to find correlation. The other option is pairwise.

table() is a good way to look at the frequency distribution.

```
> table(ct$FCS)
  0  1  2  3  4  5  6  7  8  9 10 11 12 13 14 15 16
 91 56 46 43 34 29 20 16 13  9  8  2  6  2  2  3  1
```

One of the 381 tracts has 16 foreclosures, and 91 tracts have no foreclosures. Plots provide a more visually pleasing way to look at this data.

Descriptive Plots

```
> library(lattice)
> install.packages(latticeExtra)
> library(latticeExtra)
```

lattice and latticeExtra are useful packages for data visualization. lattice comes with generic functions to create trellis graphics, and allows extensive customization via user-control parameters. In the following examples, we take a closer look at foreclosures grouped by median household income per tract, using tools available in the lattice packages.

We can first construct a new variable that groups the median household income into two groups. Group one contains tracts that are higher than the national median household income (above $50K); group two contains tracts that are lower than national median household income:

```
> IncomeLevels<-as.factor((ct$medianHouseholdIncome)>50000)
> IncomeLevels
[1] FALSE FALSE FALSE FALSE FALSE FALSE FALSE FALSE FALSE ...
```

The IncomeLevels can then be renamed as such:

```
> levels(IncomeLevels) <- c("<50K", ">50K")
> IncomeLevels
[1] <50K <50K <50K <50K <50K <50K <50K <50K <50K ...
```

Now we can construct the plot seen in Figure 2-3:

```
> print(stripplot(IncomeLevels ~ jitter(ct$FCs),
            main = list(
              "Foreclosures grouped by National Median Household Income",
              cex=1),
            sub=list("Greater or less than $50,000", cex=1),
            xlab = "foreclosures",
            ylab=" household median income",
            aspect=.3,col="light blue", pch=2 ) +
         as.layer(bwplot(IncomeLevels ~ ct$FCs,
                    varwidth=TRUE, box.ratio=0.4, col="blue", pch="|"))
    )
```

Two graphical functions are used in this case: stripplot() and bwplot(). stripplot plots each number of foreclosures per tract, while bwplot provides a boxplot. The + between the two functions tells R that the graph is not complete, and as.layer() allows us to overlay the boxplot over the stripplot. We also have the ability to change the labels and the size of the points and boxes.

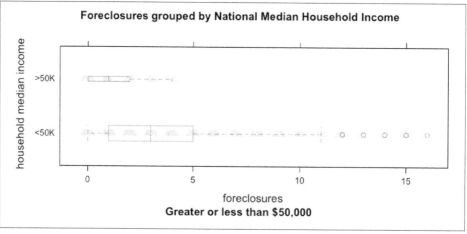

Figure 2-3. A combination of stripplot and boxplot that graphically demonstrates the household median income of the two groups

Correlation

Can we find any associations between the attributes of each tract and its foreclosures? Correlation is a basic statistic used frequently by researchers and statisticians. In R, we can create multidimensional correlation graphs using the `pairs()` scatterplot matrix package. The following code will enhance `pairs()` by allowing the upper triangle to show the actual correlation numbers, while the lower triangle will show correlation plots:

```
#make a subset of the table that only includes covariates and foreclosures
> corTable1<-ct[,c(18,20,21,22,23,24,25,27,28,31)]
#first create a function (panel.cor) for the upper triangle
> panel.cor <- function(x, y, digits=3, prefix="", cex.cor){
    usr <- par("usr"); on.exit(par(usr))
    par(usr = c(0, 1, 0, 1))
    r = (cor(x, y, method="pearson", use="complete"))
    txt <- format(c(r, 0.123456789), digits=digits)[1]
    txt <- paste(prefix, txt, sep="")
    if(missing(cex.cor)) cex <- 0.8/strwidth(txt)
    text(0.5, 0.5, txt, cex = cex * abs(r))
  }

#now plot using pairs()
> pairs(corTable1, lower.panel=panel.smooth,
    upper.panel=panel.cor, main="2009 Housing Census Data",
    labels=c("TotPop","Families","NonFamilies","TravelTime","TT+90",
     "Disabled","Income","Poverty","Occupied","FCS")
     , font.labels=2)
```

The resulting graph is shown in Figure 2-4.

In this plot, we observe that total population, total families households, and total housing units are all highly correlated (as would be expected). We also observe that median household income, total travel time, number of occupants below poverty level, and number of non-family households are not correlated with each other or any of the other variables. One interesting observation is the correlation between the total population and the median household income.

There are one or two less populated tracts whose household income is also quite high, while the remainder follow a linear trend. The median household income appears constant across all tracts regardless of the total population in each tract. For other variables, the tracts with a high number of individuals below the poverty level tend to have median household incomes at the lower end of the range. Such a clumping trend is also observed between those with low income. There is a non-linear relationship between foreclosure rates and median income, where tracts above a certain income threshold experience almost no foreclosure events.

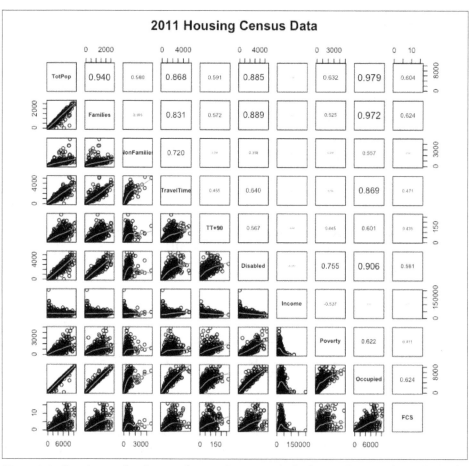

Figure 2-4. Correlation plot that simultaneously outputs both the correlation value and plot for multiple covariates

Final Thoughts

R users rely on packages to do complex tasks without heavy scripting. Using these packages effectively often requires some trial and error, but R package usage patterns will typically resemble what has been covered in this tutorial. In addition to reviewing the internal help and examples, it is good practice to closely examine each package's data structures using str(). The interactive nature of R allows a beginner to attempt to solve complex problems by trying different strategies in real-time, without the hassles of compilation. A spatial mashup cannot cover R's extensive statistical capabilities, but hopefully this book will spark some interest in programmers who want to incorporate statistical analysis into their data pipelines.

Getting Started

Obtaining R

R is available here: *http://cran.r-project.org/.*

Consoles with a limited but handy menu come with the Windows and Mac distributions. These make it somewhat easier to browse available packages and documentation. In Unix, the R executable will generally install into /usr/bin/R and uses the X Window System (X11) for graphs.

The commands in this book work for all R platforms.

Quick and Dirty Essentials of R

Upon starting R, you will see a prompt describing the version of R you are accessing, a disclaimer about R as a free software, and some functions regarding license, contributors, and demos of R.

R uses an interactive shell—each line is interpreted after you hit return. A > prompt appears when R is ready for another command. In this book, all commands that a user enters appear in bold after the prompt.

Built-in functions and simple mathematical calculations are the basics of R language. By typing 1+1 and hitting Enter, you'll observe the following:

```
> 1+1
[1] 2

> myAnswer<-sqrt(81)
> myAnswer
 [1] 9
```

Just like a calculator, you can also take logs with log(), find the sin of angles with sin(), and take absolute values of any real number with abs(). R allows you to store your results in a variable by using the <- operator. To view the value of a variable, simply type its name. Names in R are case-sensitive, so one, One, and oNe are three different variables. You can also create a vector (a collection of elements) using variables of the same type (int, num, etc):

```
> x<-c(0,1,2,3)  # R treats everything behind the pound sign as comments x [1] 0 1 2 3
```

```
> x[1]  #access to the first element of the vector [1] 0
```

To view the internal help page for a unfamiliar function, type the keyword with ?. It will provide a detailed description of the function, its parameters, its outputs, and is generally followed by a simple example using the function. You can also type help.search() to determine if there is a function that will perform what you desire.

```
> ?mean
> help.search(mean)
```

O'Reilly Resources

If you would like to learn about R in more detail, we recommend these other O'Reilly titles:

- R in a Nutshell, by Joseph Adler
- R Cookbook, by Paul Teetor
- 25 Recipes for Getting Started with R, also by Paul Teetor

Get even more for your money.

The information you need, when and where you need it.

With Safari Books Online, you can:

Access the contents of thousands of technology and business books

- Quickly search over 7000 books and certification guides
- Download whole books or chapters in PDF format, at no extra cost, to print or read on the go
- Copy and paste code
- Save up to 35% on O'Reilly print books
- **New!** Access mobile-friendly books directly from cell phones and mobile devices

Stay up-to-date on emerging topics before the books are published

- Get on-demand access to evolving manuscripts.
- Interact directly with authors of upcoming books

Explore thousands of hours of video on technology and design topics

- Learn from expert video tutorials
- Watch and replay recorded conference sessions

Spreading the knowledge of innovators   safari.oreilly.com

Ingram Content Group UK Ltd.
Milton Keynes UK
UKHW031951210323
418937UK00010B/586